HOW DOES IT FLY?
BLIMP

BY SHARON NITTINGER

Published in the United States of America by Cherry Lake Publishing
Ann Arbor, Michigan
www.cherrylakepublishing.com

Content Adviser: Jacob Zeiger, Production Support Engineer, the Boeing Company

Special thanks to Rob Delagrange, Goodyear blimp pilot, for sharing his time, knowledge, and support in the writing of this book.

Photo Credits: Cover and pages 1, 5, 7, 9, 11, 13, and 21, Photos courtesy of The Goodyear Tire & Rubber Company; page 15, ©First Light/Alamy; page 17, ©Kenneth Summers/Shutterstock, Inc.; page 19, ©Kenneth Sponsler/Shutterstock, Inc.

LIBRARY OF CONGRESS CATALOGING-IN-PUBLICATION DATA
Nittinger, Sharon, 1966–
  How does it fly? Blimp/by Sharon Nittinger.
    p. cm.—(Community connections)
  Includes bibliographical references and index.
  ISBN-13: 978-1-61080-071-6 (lib. bdg.)
  ISBN-10: 1-61080-071-0 (lib. bdg.)
  1. Airships—Juvenile literature. I. Title. II. Title: Blimp.
  TL650.5.N58 2011
  629.133'27—dc22   2010051213

Cherry Lake Publishing would like to acknowledge the work of The Partnership for 21st Century Skills. Please visit www.21stcenturyskills.org for more information.

Printed in the United States of America
Corporate Graphics Inc.
July 2011
CLFA09

BLIMP

CONTENTS

HOW DOES IT FLY?

LIGHTER THAN AIR

Have you ever wondered what it would feel like to float on a cloud? Riding in a blimp is like sitting on a cloud. A blimp gently floats in the sky.

4

The Goodyear blimp is one of the most recognized blimps.

What happens when you fill a balloon with air? It lies on the ground. A balloon filled with **helium** floats up. Helium is a gas that is lighter than air.

A blimp is filled with helium and air. The helium makes the blimp lighter than the outside air. This makes the blimp float up.

This blimp is being filled with helium. It is already starting to float.

Blimps are dirigibles. Hot air balloons are not dirigibles. Ask a librarian to help you learn why a hot air balloon is not a dirigible.

7

PARTS OF A BLIMP

Blimps are airships. An airship has a big bag called an envelope. The envelope gets its shape when it is filled with helium and air.

The envelope is made of sturdy material. Nose cone battens are long metal rods. They help support the front of the blimp.

Nose cone battens help a blimp's nose keep its shape.

Under the envelope is the **gondola**. The gondola is the place where the pilot and passengers sit. Engines are on both sides of the gondola. They help fly the blimp.

This blimp rises higher in the sky as it flies over a field.

A gondola is about the size of a minivan. How many people do you think a gondola can carry at one time? Look up the answer at the library or on the Internet. Did you guess correctly?

CONTROLLING A BLIMP

The pilot can move the blimp in any direction. Large, flat fins are attached to the rear of the blimp. The fins have parts called **elevators** and **rudders**. Elevators move the blimp's nose up or down. Rudders turn the blimp to the right or left.

A pilot controls elevators and rudders from inside the gondola.

13

A crew stays on the ground. These people help launch and land the blimp.

The pilot directs the blimp downward to land. An elevator wheel controls the blimp's elevators. The pilot rolls the wheel forward. This directs the blimp's nose down. Power from the blimp's engines move the airship toward the ground.

14

This blimp's crew rushes into position as the blimp lands.

Weather is important when flying a blimp. Heat from the sun warms the helium. This makes the blimp float higher. When clouds cover the sun, the blimp cools and lowers. Why do you think this is important for pilots to remember?

15

When the blimp is low enough, crew members grab the nose lines. Nose lines are two large ropes hanging from the blimp.

One crew member grabs a cable, or pendant line, attached to the ship's nose. The pendant line is tied to a low tower called a **mooring mast**. Then the blimp's nose is locked to the mooring mast.

16

The mooring mast keeps the blimp from floating away. The ship can move as the wind blows.

Watch a balloon filled with helium. Is the balloon tied to something heavy? This stops the balloon from being blown away by the wind. This is like a blimp locked to the mooring mast.

HOW BLIMPS ARE USED

Most blimps are painted with company names on the envelope. They are like flying advertisements. Have you ever watched a blimp flying over a sporting event? A special camera attached to the blimp films the sporting event. Then people can watch the event on television.

Have you ever seen a blimp fly over as you watched a sports game?

Some people use blimps for sightseeing. Tourists can look out the windows.

Blimps move very slowly. Airplanes fly much faster than blimps. Maybe you would enjoy riding in a blimp someday!

Blimps move slowly, letting tourists get a good look at the scenery.

Blimps can do things that airplanes, helicopters, and trucks cannot. Blimps can travel long distances with little fuel. They do not pollute the air as much as airplanes do. What are some new ways we could use blimps?

GLOSSARY

airships (AIR-ships) lighter than air aircraft

elevators (EL-uh-vay-torz) fins that direct a blimp up or down

envelope (EN-vuh-lohp) large bag that holds helium and air and gives the blimp its shape

gondola (GAHN-doh-luh) cabin attached under the envelope that carries passengers and the pilot

helium (HEE-lee-um) gas that is lighter than air and will not burn

mooring mast (MOR-ing MAST) small tower or post used to secure a blimp after landing

nose cone battens (NOZE KONE BAT-enz) supports for the blimp nose and used to moor the blimp

rudders (RUH-durz) fins that direct a blimp to the right or left

FIND OUT MORE

BOOKS

Galvin, Laura Gates. *First Look at Aircraft.* Washington, DC: Trudy Corporation and the Smithsonian Institution, 2009.

Hodgkins, Fran. *How People Learned to Fly.* New York: HarperCollins, 2007.

WEB SITES

Goodyear Blimp

www.goodyearblimp.com
Read about the history of the Goodyear blimp and how a blimp is made.

Modern Airships

www.modern-airships.info/en/home.html
Look at many cool pictures of all different kinds of airships, including blimps.

INDEX

24

ABOUT THE AUTHOR

Sharon Nittinger lives near the Winoot Lake Hangar in Ohio, which is home to the Goodyear Airship Operations. The Goodyear blimp frequently flies over her house, providing excitement for Sharon, her husband, Bill, and their two children. This is her second book for Cherry Lake Publishing.